# Contents

About this book with
Foreword by Archbishop Vincent Nichols (Westminster) — 3

Heart speaks unto heart — 6
Group session recalling the theme of the Papal Visit

Seeking unity — 10
Group session reflecting on the call to Christian unity

Be saints for the 21st century — 15
Group session on the possibility of living a holy life

The Kingdom of God is very near to you! — 20
Group session on spreading the Gospel through loving action

Focus on Christ — 24
Group session on the Son of God, source of all joy

Towards the common good — 28
Group session on the need for dialogue between Church and society

Daily Prayers — 33
Prayers from Sunday to Saturday

Supplementary resources including — 48
Selected writings of Pope Benedict XVI and an annotated list of popes

Faithful pilgrim

Faithful Pilgrim
978-0-9563514-7-0

Writing Group: Ms Diana Klein, Dr Mark Nash, Fr Michael O'Boy

The Diocese of Westminster's Agency for Evangelisation is grateful to the National Council of the Churches of Christ in the U.S.A for use of the New Revised Standard Version Bible: Catholic Edition copyright © 1993 and 1989. Excerpts from The Divine Office © 1974, hierarchies of Australia, England and Wales, Ireland. All rights reserved.

This booklet contains images © Mazur/catholicchurch.org.uk Used with permission

Produced by Agency for Evangelisation, Vaughan House, 46 Francis Street, London, SW1P 1QN. Tel: 020 7798 9152; email: evangelisation@rcdow.org.uk

 booklets are published by WRCDT. Design by Mark Nash. Print arranged by Transform Management Ltd info@1025transform.co.uk

Copyright © 2011, Diocese of Westminster, Archbishop's House, Ambrosden Avenue, London, SW1P 1QJ. All rights reserved.

 The Diocese of Westminster's Agency for Evangelisation is committed to a sustainable future for our planet. The booklet in your hands is made from paper certified by the Forest Stewardship Council.

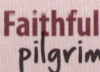

Foreword

Each of us will have our own memories of Pope Benedict's State visit to England, Scotland and Wales in September 2010. Among my own will be the welcome the Holy Father received from the young people gathered outside Westminster Cathedral, the reverent silence that filled Hyde Park during Exposition of the Blessed Sacrament, and, more personally, the privilege of accompanying Pope Benedict in the popemobile.

Quite possibly you were one of those hundreds of thousands who welcomed the Holy Father on the streets, or you were able to attend one of the celebrations in Glasgow, Westminster and Birmingham. And if you were not able to attend, perhaps you watched from home sharing in the joy of welcoming the Holy Father and the pride we all felt as he reached out to all the members of our society, believers and unbelievers alike.

I could not hope to list all the graces that have flowed as a result of the Holy Father's visit. It was after all a particularly rich diet with so much to take in, in such a short space of time. And this, in simple terms, is the reasoning behind this faith sharing resource. Here, we will be invited to reflect more closely on what Pope Benedict said to us during his visit. More particularly, we will focus on some of his central themes: the riches of our Christian faith, the contribution we can and should make to the well being of society, and the more personal challenge of living our faith in our own individual circumstances. In committing yourself to this time of faith sharing, my prayer is that the graces we experienced during the Holy Father's visit will flow ever deeper, and that our joy, as bearers of the Good News, will shine more brightly.

Yours devotedly,

+ Vincent Nichols

The Most Reverend Vincent Nichols
Archbishop of Westminster

About this book

'In the four busy and very beautiful days I spent in this noble land I had the great joy of speaking to the hearts of the inhabitants of the United Kingdom and they spoke to mine, especially with their presence and with the testimony of their faith. Indeed I could see how strong the Christian heritage still is and how active it still is in social life at every level. British hearts and British lives are open to the reality of God.' (*General Audience, 22 September 2010, St Peter's Square*).

Reflecting on his own visit to the United Kingdom on his return to Rome, the Holy Father talked of his desire to support and encourage Catholics in placing the gospel at the root of society. He spoke too of his wish to speak to the hearts of all the inhabitants of the United Kingdom, 'excluding no one, of the true reality of man, of his deepest needs, of his ultimate destiny.' [for the full reflection visit: http://tinyurl.com/220910audience].

The six group sessions of this booklet offer each of us the opportunity to reflect on this historic visit together. It follows the same format as *Hail Mary, Full of Grace* [This can be downloaded from http://issuu.com/exploringfaith/docs/hailmary]. This resource draws its title from the Pope's own claim that he came as a pilgrim to our nation and serves as a call to us all, to be faithful pilgrims in the world today.

The group sessions are supplemented by additional materials and text boxes on the encyclicals of Pope Benedict XVI, an annotated list of Popes and information on the symbols and insignia of papal office. The booklet is illustrated with many photos which may serve to stir a thought in a way that the text could not. We also invite you to make use of the daily prayers in the second half of the booklet which are drawn from the Divine Office.

This booklet is not tied to a particular time of year and the prayers and meditations may be used by individuals, groups or in a wider parish context throughout the year. Additional reflections and thoughts can be found on our small group blog - *a threefold cord is not easily broken* [http://dowsmallgroups.wordpress.com].

Your parish will have been provided with a 'visit' candle and a copy of Holman Hunt's 'Light of the World', you may wish to ask your parish priest if you can borrow these for the focal point of your time together. More on the image and prayers for use with it can be found at http://www.thepapalvisit.org.uk/legacy.

Faithful pilgrim

Heart speaks unto heart

session one

Opening Prayers
Taken from the Songs of Solomon 8:6-7

Leader: Set me as a seal upon your heart,
as a seal upon your arm;

Group: for love is strong as death,
passion fierce as the grave.

Leader: Its flashes are flashes of fire,
a raging flame.

Group: Many waters cannot quench love,
neither can floods drown it.

Leader: If one offered for love
all the wealth of one's house,
it would be utterly scorned.

All: Glory be to the Father, and to the Son and to the Holy Spirit. As it was in the beginning, is now, and ever shall be, world without end. Amen.

For a few moments, either aloud or in the silence of our hearts, let us give thanks to the Lord for all the blessings we have received over the past week. As we give thanks let us remember, again in silence or aloud, all those who need our prayers. Keeping in mind God's mercy, let us remember all the times that we have turned from him and ask for his forgiveness.

Introduction to the Scripture reading
Let us listen carefully to the Word of the Lord,
and attend to it with the ear of our hearts.
Let us welcome it, and faithfully put it into practice.

St. Benedict of Nursia (c.480-c.547) adapted

Faithful pilgrim

Explore the Scriptures 1 John 4:7-15, 18-19

Beloved, let us love one another, because love is from God; everyone who loves is born of God and knows God. Whoever does not love does not know God, for God is love. God's love was revealed among us in this way: God sent his only Son into the world so that we might live through him. In this is love, not that we loved God but that he loved us and sent his Son to be the atoning sacrifice for our sins. Beloved, since God loved us so much, we also ought to love one another. No one has ever seen God; if we love one another, God lives in us, and his love is perfected in us.

By this we know that we abide in him and he in us, because he has given us of his Spirit. And we have seen and do testify that the Father has sent his Son as the Saviour of the world. God abides in those who confess that Jesus is the Son of God, and they abide in God. There is no fear in love, but perfect love casts out fear; for fear has to do with punishment, and whoever fears has not reached perfection in love. We love because he first loved us. Those who say, 'I love God', and hate their brothers or sisters, are liars; for those who do not love a brother or sister whom they have seen, cannot love God whom they have not seen.

Please take a few moments in silence to reflect on the passage, then share a word or phrase that has struck you. Pause to think about what others have said then, after a second reading of the passage, you may wish to share a further thought.

Reflection

For many years Joseph Ratzinger, now Pope Benedict XVI, has had great respect and a deep fascination with the thought and writings of Blessed John Henry Newman. As a rule, beatification ceremonies are carried out by the local bishop but the Holy Father insisted on performing the rites for Cardinal Newman. As the theme for the visit the Pope chose the words Heart speaks unto heart – the words on Cardinal Newman's crest, in Latin *Cor ad cor loquitur*. Throughout the papal visit to the United Kingdom the Holy Father echoed this motto, returning time and

again to the themes of love, both of God and neighbour, and dialogue, with God through prayer and with those seeking what is right.

Speaking to the young people gathered outside of Westminster Cathedral the Holy Father asked them to open their hearts and to think of the love their hearts were made to both give and to receive. 'After all,' said the Holy Father, 'we were made for love'. 'This,' he continued, 'is what the Bible means when it says that we are made in the image and likeness of God (Genesis 1:26). We were made to know the God of love, the God who is Father, Son and Holy Spirit, and to find our supreme fulfilment in that Divine love that knows no beginning or end.'

Reminding us that we were made to receive love, Pope Benedict asked us to give thanks to God for the love we have known; 'the love that has made us who we are...that (has) shown us what is truly important in life...the love we have received from our families, our friends, our teachers, and all those people in our lives who have helped us to realise how precious we are in their eyes, and in the eyes of God.'

Calling to mind those times when it is easy to love, those times when 'our hearts brim over with generosity, idealism [and] the desire to help others to build a better world' the Holy Father reminded us that sometimes, despite our being made to love, having love as our constant inspiration can be difficult: 'our hearts can easily be hardened by selfishness, envy and pride.'

Looking to Blessed Mother Theresa of Calcutta, Pope Benedict reminded us, as she did, that loving is the fruit of a daily decision which requires the help of Christ. 'Every day we have to choose to love and this requires help. This help that comes from Christ, from the wisdom found in his word and from the Grace which he bestows on us in the sacraments of his Church.' For Pope Benedict the key to loving lies in the discovery of Christ. 'I ask you,' he said,' to look into your hearts, each day, to find the source of all true love. Jesus is always there. Quietly waiting for us to be still with him and to hear his voice… even amidst the business and stress of our daily lives we need to make space for silence, because it is in silence that we

Heart speaks unto heart
When Newman became a cardinal in 1879, he had to choose a motto to go on his coat of arms. He chose the Latin words Cor ad Cor loquitur – heart speaks unto heart. Where did these words come from? At the time, Newman thought they came from the Imitation of Christ (written by Thomas à Kempis in the 1400s), but in fact he was mistaken – they are from St Francis de Sales (1567-1622), a French bishop and great spiritual writer whom Newman revered. Newman chose to put a painting of St Francis above the altar in his own chapel at the Birmingham Oratory.

find God. In silence that we discover our true self. And, in discovering our true self, we discover the particular vocation which God has given us for the building up of his Church and the redemption of our world. Heart speaks unto heart.'

What part does silence play in my prayer? Where do I take the time to listen to what Christ might be saying to me? Where, in the business of daily living, could I find space for silence?

Closing Prayers
You may wish to end this session with some different prayers, the Our Father or silent reflection.

Lord, source of eternal life and truth,
give to your shepherd, Pope Benedict,
a spirit of courage, knowledge and love.
By governing with fidelity those entrusted to his care,
may he, as successor to the apostle Peter,
help the Church be a sign of unity, love, and peace.
We ask this through your Son, Jesus Christ,
who lives and reigns with you and the Holy Spirit,
one God, for ever and ever.
Amen.

The full text of Pope Benedict XVI's address to young people on the Westminster Cathedral piazza and his homily in the Cathedral can be found on the Papal Visit website: http://www.thepapalvisit.org.uk/speeches.

If you have the time you may wish to print out the homily and read a paragraph each day in the week ahead.

Notes

Seeking unity

session two

Opening Prayers
Taken from St Paul's letter to the Ephesians 4:1-15

Leader: Lord, we humbly ask that we be made worthy
of the life to which you have called us,
grant us humility and gentleness,
help us to bear with one another in love,
making every effort to maintain
the unity of the Spirit in the bond of peace.

Group: There is one body and one Spirit,
there is one Lord, one faith, one baptism,
one God and Father of all,
who is above all and through all and in all.

Leader: Each of us was given grace
according to the measure of Christ's gift.

Group: The gifts he gave were that some would be apostles,
some prophets, some evangelists,
some pastors and teachers,
to equip the saints for the work of ministry,
for building up the body of Christ,

Leader: until all of us come to the unity of the faith
and of the knowledge of the Son of God,
to maturity, to the measure of the full stature of Christ.

Group: Grant that we no longer be children,
but speaking the truth in love,
may we grow up in every way into him
who is the head, into Christ. Amen.

For a few moments, either aloud or in the silence of our hearts, let us give thanks to the Lord for all the blessings we have received over the past week. As we give thanks let us remember, again in silence or aloud, all those who need our prayers. Keeping in mind God's mercy, let us remember all the times that we have turned from him and ask for his forgiveness.

Introduction to Reading of Scripture
Let us listen carefully to the Word of the Lord,
and attend to it with the ear of our hearts.
Let us welcome it, and faithfully put it into practice.

St. Benedict of Nursia (c.480-c.547) adapted

Explore the Scriptures John 10:1-18
'Very truly, I tell you, anyone who does not enter the sheepfold by the gate but climbs in by another way is a thief and a bandit. The one who enters by the gate is the shepherd of the sheep. The gatekeeper opens the gate for him, and the sheep hear his voice. He calls his own sheep by name and leads them out. When he has brought out all his own, he goes ahead of them, and the sheep follow him because they know his voice. They will not follow a stranger, but they will run from him because they do not know the voice of strangers.' Jesus used this figure of speech with them, but they did not understand what he was saying to them.

So again Jesus said to them, 'Very truly, I tell you, I am the gate for the sheep. All who came before me are thieves and bandits; but the sheep did not listen to them. I am the gate. Whoever enters by me will be saved, and will come in and go out and find pasture. The thief comes only to steal and kill and destroy. I came that they may have life, and have it abundantly.

'I am the good shepherd. The good shepherd lays down his life for the sheep. The hired hand, who is not the shepherd and does not own the sheep, sees the wolf coming and leaves the sheep and runs away – and the wolf snatches them and scatters them. The hired hand runs away because a hired hand does not care for the sheep. I am the good shepherd. I know my own and my own know me, just as the Father knows me and I know the Father. And I lay down my life for the sheep. I have other sheep that do not belong to this fold. I must bring them also, and they will listen to my voice. So there will be one flock, one shepherd. For this reason the Father loves me, because I lay down my life in order to take it up again. No one takes it from me, but I lay it down of my own accord. I have power to lay it down, and I have power to take it up again. I have received this command from my Father.'

Please take a few moments in silence to reflect on the passage, then share a word or phrase that has struck you. Pause to think about what others have said then after a second reading of the passage you may wish to share a further thought.

Reflection

Before flying back to Rome, Pope Benedict XVI reflected on the success of his visit and reminded the bishops of England, Scotland and Wales to 'present in its fullness the life-giving message of the gospel' and to 'encourage people to aspire to higher moral values in every area of their lives, against a background of growing cynicism regarding even the possibility of virtuous living'. The Holy Father also outlined two priorities: the new translation of the Missal and the recent document on receiving Anglicans into full communion with the Catholic Church.

This document, *Anglicanorum Coetibus*, should be seen as a 'prophetic gesture', remarked the Pope, 'that can contribute positively to the ultimate goal of all ecumenical activity: the restoration of full ecclesial communion.' For the Holy Father, such activity is to be characterised by a 'mutual exchange of gifts from our respective spiritual patrimonies which will serve to enrich us all.'

The goal of communion and Christian Unity has been a recurring theme of Pope Benedict XVI's pontificate. Initially commentators remarked on his desire for reconciliation with the Churches of the East, but the Holy Father's focus was not restricted just to these. At his inauguration he recalled the words of Christ: 'I have other sheep that are not of this fold; I must lead them too, and they will heed my voice. So there shall be one flock, one shepherd' (John 10:16). The day after his election, addressing the Cardinal Electors, the Pope spoke of Christ's expression of hope for the unity of those who believe in him. For his part, the Pope 'knows that he must make himself especially responsible for his Divine Master's supreme aspiration… This is his ambition, his impelling duty. He is aware that good intentions do not suffice for this. Concrete gestures that enter hearts and stir consciences are essential, inspiring in everyone that inner conversion that is the prerequisite for all ecumenical progress.' As the Holy Father has a role in serving the unity of the Church so do we: 'each one of us must come before Christ, the supreme Judge of every living person, and render an account to him of all we

have done or have failed to do to further the great good of the full and visible unity of all his disciples.'

The service of Evening Prayer at Westminster Abbey provided the perfect platform for a reaffirmation of such a message. 'Our commitment to Christian unity is born of nothing less than our faith in Christ, in this Christ, risen from the dead and seated at the right hand of the Father, who will come again in glory to judge the living and the dead… We are aware of the disappointments and the signs of hope that have marked our ecumenical journey. We know the friendships we have forged, the dialogue we have begun. We must also recognise the challenges that confront us along the path of Christian unity and also in our task of proclaiming Christ in our day… May the Risen Lord strengthen our efforts to mend the ruptures of the past and to meet the challenges of the present with hope in the future which, in his providence, he holds out to us and to our world.'

What prejudices am I conscious of when relating to Christians from other traditions? What 'concrete gestures' have I made and could I make to serve the unity of Christians? How might Christian reconciliation aid the cause of Christian witness in this country?

Closing Prayers
You may wish to end this session with some different prayers, the Our Father or silent reflection.

Lord, source of eternal life and truth,
give to your shepherd, Pope Benedict,
a spirit of courage, knowledge and love.
By governing with fidelity those entrusted to his care,
may he, as successor to the apostle Peter,
help the Church be a sign of unity, love, and peace.
We ask this through your Son, Jesus Christ,
who lives and reigns with you and the Holy Spirit,
one God, for ever and ever.
Amen.

 **Notes**

Adoration of the Trinity (also known as Landaur Altar) by Albrecht Dürer (1511)

Be saints for the 21st century
session three

Opening prayer
Taken from the letter to the Hebrews 12:1-13

Leader: Since we are surrounded by so great a cloud of witnesses,
let us lay aside every weight and the sin that clings so closely.

Group: Let us run with perseverance the race that is set before us,
looking to Jesus the pioneer and perfecter of our faith,

Leader: who endured the cross,
and has taken his seat at the right hand of God.

Group: Let us endure trials for the sake of discipline,
though discipline always seems painful
rather than pleasant at the time,
it later yields the peaceful fruit of righteousness.

Leader: Let us lift our drooping hands
and strengthen our weak knees.

Group: Let us pray to the Lord
that he make straight paths for our feet,
And heal in us what is lame

All: Glory be to the Father, and to the Son and to the Holy Spirit. As it was in the beginning, is now, and ever shall be, world without end. Amen.

For a few moments, either aloud or in the silence of our hearts, let us give thanks to the Lord for all the blessings we have received over the past week. As we give thanks let us remember, again in silence or aloud, all those who need our prayers. Keeping in mind God's mercy, let us remember all the times that we have turned from him and ask for his forgiveness.

Faithful pilgrim

Introduction to Reading of Scripture
Let us listen carefully to the Word of the Lord,
and attend to it with the ear of our hearts.
Let us welcome it, and faithfully put it into practice.

St. Benedict of Nursia (c.480-c.547) adapted

Explore the Scriptures Philippians 4:4-13
Rejoice in the Lord always; again I will say, Rejoice. Let your gentleness be known to everyone. The Lord is near. Do not worry about anything, but in everything, by prayer and supplication with thanksgiving, let your requests be made known to God. And the peace of God, which surpasses all understanding, will guard your hearts and your minds in Christ Jesus.

Finally, beloved, whatever is true, whatever is honourable, whatever is just, whatever is pure, whatever is pleasing, whatever is commendable, if there is any excellence and if there is anything worthy of praise, think about these things. Keep on doing the things that you have learned and received and heard and seen in me, and the God of peace will be with you.

I rejoice in the Lord greatly that now at last you have revived your concern for me; indeed, you were concerned for me, but had no opportunity to show it. Not that I am referring to being in need; for I have learned to be content with whatever I have. I know what it is to have little, and I know what it is to have plenty. In any and all circumstances I have learned the secret of being well-fed and of going hungry, of having plenty and of being in need. I can do all things through him who strengthens me.

Please take a few moments in silence to reflect on the passage, then share a word or phrase that has struck you. Pause to think about what others have said then after a second reading of the passage you may wish to share a further thought.

Reflection
Up and down the country, Catholic schoolchildren had their lessons suspended on Friday morning, 19 September 2010 and were allowed to watch screens featuring a live feed from Twickenham, where the Holy Father was holding what was called 'The Big Assembly'. His address to the thousands of pupils gathered at St Mary's, Strawberry Hill, and over the internet, was a true highlight of this visit which captivated and engaged people of all ages and from all walks of life. Speaking to these pupils, from all over the U.K, Pope Benedict expressed the hope that some of them would be among the future saints of the twenty-first century.

Taking up his theme, the Holy Father asked the young people before him to consider the qualities they saw in others which they would most like to see in themselves. However, conscious of the tendency to model ourselves on the rich and the famous, the entertainer and the sportsman, the Holy Father asked his audience not to be short sighted in the setting and pursuit of their goals:

'When I invite you to become saints', he said, 'I am asking you not to be content with second best…to pursue one limited goal and ignore all the others. Having money,' he explains, 'makes it possible to be generous and to do good in the world, but on its own, it is not enough to make us happy. Being highly skilled in some activity or profession is good, but it will not satisfy us unless we aim for something greater still. It might make us famous, but it will not make us happy.'

For the Pope one of the greatest tragedies is our ability to search for happiness in the wrong places. True happiness, he insists, is to be found in God. 'We need to have the courage to place our deepest hopes in God alone, not in money, in a career, in worldly success, or in our relationships with others, but in God. Only he can satisfy the deepest needs of our hearts.'

Implicit in all that the Holy Father has to say is a direct link between the holiness we associate with saintliness and our being happy. They are, as it were, two sides of the same coin. 'God', as Pope Benedict puts it, 'loves you more than you could ever begin to imagine, and he wants the very best for you. And by far the best thing for you is to grow in holiness'. It is for this reason that God, in the Holy Father's words, wants our friendship – wants to discover in us a way of life that is attractive to him and transforming for us.

'As you come to know him better, you find you want to reflect something of his infinite goodness… You begin to see greed and selfishness and all sins for what

Pay attention to the bigger picture

The Holy Father also paid close attention to the role of Catholic education in society, and in the education of the whole person.

'Never allow yourselves to become narrow. The world needs good scientists, but a scientific outlook becomes dangerously narrow if it ignores the religious or ethical dimension of life, just as religion becomes narrow if it rejects the legitimate contribution of science to our understanding of the world. We need good historians, philosophers and economists, but if their account of human life is too narrowly focussed, they can lead us astray. A bigger picture exists.'

You may be interested in reading Pope John Paul II's encyclical on the relationship between faith and reason – *Fides et ratio* (1998)

they really are, destructive and dangerous tendencies that cause deep suffering and do great damage, and you want to avoid falling into that trap yourselves. You begin to feel compassion for people in difficulties and are eager to do something to help them. You want to come to the aid of the poor and the hungry, comfort the sorrowful; you want to be kind and generous. And, once these things begin to matter to you, you are well on the way to becoming saints.'

What do you look for in a saint? What cause, what issue, what injustice **really** *matters to you today? Imagine that you were declared a saint tomorrow, of what would you want to be the patron saint and why?*

Closing Prayers
You may wish to end this session with some different prayers, the Our Father or silent reflection.

Lord, source of eternal life and truth,
give to your shepherd, Pope Benedict,
a spirit of courage, knowledge and love.
By governing with fidelity those entrusted to his care,
may he, as successor to the apostle Peter,
help the Church be a sign of unity, love, and peace.
We ask this through your Son, Jesus Christ,
who lives and reigns with you and the Holy Spirit,
one God, for ever and ever.
Amen.

Notes

Think about... praying for all of those people, alive and departed, who promoted your knowledge of the faith.

The Kingdom of God is very near to you!

session four

Opening prayer
Taken from Psalm 144(145)

Leader: I will extol you, my God and King,
and bless your name for ever and ever.
Every day I will bless you,
and praise your name for ever and ever.

Group: One generation shall laud your works to another,
and shall declare your mighty acts.
They shall celebrate the fame of your abundant goodness,
and shall sing aloud of your righteousness.

Leader: The Lord is gracious and merciful,
slow to anger and abounding in steadfast love.
The Lord is good to all,
and his compassion is over all that he has made.

Group: All your works shall give thanks to you, O Lord,
and all your faithful shall bless you.
They shall speak of the glory of your kingdom,
and tell of your power,
to make known to all people your mighty deeds,
and the glorious splendour of your kingdom.

Leader: Your kingdom is an everlasting kingdom,
and your dominion endures throughout all generations.

All: Glory be to the Father, and to the Son and to the Holy Spirit. As it was in the beginning, is now, and ever shall be, world without end. Amen.

For a few moments, either aloud or in the silence of our hearts, let us give thanks to the Lord for all the blessings we have received over the past week. As we give thanks let us remember, again in silence or aloud, all those who need our prayers. Keeping in mind God's mercy, let us remember all the times that we have turned from him and ask for his forgiveness.

Faithful pilgrim

Introduction to Reading of Scripture
Let us listen carefully to the Word of the Lord,
and attend to it with the ear of our hearts.
Let us welcome it, and faithfully put it into practice.

St. Benedict of Nursia (c.480-c.547) adapted

Explore the Scriptures Luke 10:1-9
After this the Lord appointed seventy others and sent them on ahead of him in pairs to every town and place where he himself intended to go. He said to them, 'The harvest is plentiful, but the labourers are few; therefore ask the Lord of the harvest to send out labourers into his harvest. Go on your way. See, I am sending you out like lambs into the midst of wolves. Carry no purse, no bag, no sandals; and greet no one on the road. Whatever house you enter, first say, "Peace to this house!" And if anyone is there who shares in peace, your peace will rest on that person; but if not, it will return to you. Remain in the same house, eating and drinking whatever they provide, for the labourer deserves to be paid. Do not move about from house to house. Whenever you enter a town and its people welcome you, eat what is set before you; cure the sick who are there, and say to them, "The kingdom of God has come near to you."

Please take a few moments in silence to reflect on the passage, then share a word or phrase that has struck you. Pause to think about what others have said then after a second reading of the passage you may wish to share a further thought.

Reflection
Ever since the very first years of the Church, solidarity with and concern for those in need has been a cornerstone for our faith and a sure sign of the building of Christ's Kingdom. The need to work for what is right, called for by Our Lord in his Sermon on the Mount and enshrined in the teaching of his bride, the Church, is no less important today.

Speaking in Bellahouston Park, Pope Benedict invited us to 'reaffirm our faith in Christ's word and our hope...in his promises'. Pointing to the gospel in which Christ sent out seventy two disciples (Luke 10: 1-9) to proclaim the presence of the Kingdom, Pope Benedict reminded us that Christ sends us today 'to proclaim the coming of his Kingdom and to bring his peace into the world...house by house, family by family, town by town.'

Pope Benedict went on to say that the preaching of the gospel has always been accompanied by a concern for the Word and the culture in which it takes root and flourishes. Commenting on the task that we face today the Holy Father said the

'evangelisation of culture is all the more important' because of a 'dictatorship of relativism' which, as he puts it, 'threatens to obscure the unchanging truth about man's nature, his destiny and his ultimate good.' Countering those who would like to sideline religious faith, Pope Benedict went on to insist that 'religion is...a guarantee of authentic liberty and respect' because it leads us 'to look upon every person as a brother or sister.' Accordingly, Pope Benedict challenged us to witness to our faith and 'to put the case for the promotion of faith's wisdom and vision in the public forum'.

As Christians, we believe that the answer to all our longings is in Christ. Even so, the Holy Father's call to keep faith alive in the public forum is not born of a sectarian desire to make everyone Catholic, rather, it is rooted in a fundamental concern to serve the wellbeing of all. Writing in *Deus Caritas Est,* he reminds us 'Charity...cannot be used as a means of engaging in...proselytism. Love is free; it is not practised as a way of achieving other ends. But this does not mean that charitable activity must somehow leave God and Christ aside for it is always concerned with the whole person. Often the deepest cause of suffering is the very absence of God. Those who practise charity in the Church's name will never seek to impose the Church's faith upon others. They realise that a pure and generous love is the best witness to the God in whom we believe and by whom we are driven to love' (DCE, 31 - *more on this encyclical on p.52*)

Simply put, the life of the Church and its members should be attractive and compelling to those outside. Our lives should arouse curiosity by their goodness and encourage people to enquire as to the source of this same goodness. As the Holy Father insists, Christianity is not a list of negative proscriptions or lists of things disapproved of by the Church, but rather a positive option, a positive influence and a source of joy and life.

If you were asked for signs of Christ's presence and the Kingdom of God, what would you point to? What difficulties do you experience in treating all the people you meet as a brother or sister? What joys and challenges has your Christian faith brought to your life? Do you experience your faith as something positive?

Closing Prayers
You may wish to end this session with some different prayers, the Our Father or silent reflection.

Lord, source of eternal life and truth,
give to your shepherd, Pope Benedict,
a spirit of courage, knowledge and love.
By governing with fidelity those entrusted to his care,
may he, as successor to the apostle Peter,
help the Church be a sign of unity, love, and peace.
We ask this through your Son, Jesus Christ,
who lives and reigns with you and the Holy Spirit,
one God, for ever and ever.
Amen.

The full text of Pope Benedict XVI's homily at the Bellahouston Mass on 16 September can be found on the Papal Visit website: http://www.thepapalvisit.org.uk/speeches.

If you have the time you may wish to share your thoughts on the whole homily, or perhaps you may wish to print out the homily and read a paragraph each day in the week ahead.

 Notes

Focus on Christ

session five

Opening prayer
Taken from Psalm 23

Leader: The Lord is my shepherd, I shall not want.
He makes me lie down in green pastures;
he leads me beside still waters;
he restores my soul.

Group: He leads me in right paths
for his name's sake.

Leader: Even though I walk through the darkest valley,
I fear no evil;
for you are with me;
your rod and your staff—
they comfort me.

Group: You prepare a table before me
in the presence of my enemies;
you anoint my head with oil;
my cup overflows.

Leader: Surely goodness and mercy shall follow me
all the days of my life,
and I shall dwell in the house of the Lord
my whole life long.

All: Glory be to the Father, and to the Son and to the Holy Spirit. As it was in the beginning, is now, and ever shall be, world without end. Amen.

For a few moments, either aloud or in the silence of our hearts, let us give thanks to the Lord for all the blessings we have received over the past week. As we give thanks let us remember, again in silence or aloud, all those who need our prayers. Keeping in mind God's mercy, let us remember all the times that we have turned from him and ask for his forgiveness.

Introduction to Reading of Scripture

Let us listen carefully to the Word of the Lord,
and attend to it with the ear of our hearts.
Let us welcome it, and faithfully put it into practice.

St. Benedict of Nursia (c.480-c.547) adapted

Explore the Scriptures Colossians 2:5-17
The theme for World Youth Day 2011 in Madrid is taken from this passage

For though I am absent in body, yet I am with you in spirit, and I rejoice to see your morale and the firmness of your faith in Christ. As you therefore have received Christ Jesus the Lord, continue to live your lives in him, rooted and built up in him and established in the faith, just as you were taught, abounding in thanksgiving.

See to it that no one takes you captive through philosophy and empty deceit, according to human tradition, according to the elemental spirits of the universe, and not according to Christ. For in him the whole fullness of deity dwells bodily, and you have come to fullness in him, who is the head of every ruler and authority. In him also you were circumcised with a spiritual circumcision, by putting off the body of the flesh in the circumcision of Christ; when you were buried with him in baptism, you were also raised with him through faith in the power of God, who raised him from the dead. And when you were dead in trespasses and the uncircumcision of your flesh, God made you alive together with him, when he forgave us all our trespasses, erasing the record that stood against us with its legal demands. He set this aside, nailing it to the cross. He disarmed the rulers and authorities and made a public example of them, triumphing over them in it.

Therefore do not let anyone condemn you in matters of food and drink or of observing festivals, new moons, or sabbaths. These are only a shadow of what is to come, but the substance belongs to Christ.

Please take a few moments in silence to reflect on the passage, then share a word or phrase that has struck you. Pause to think about what others have said then after a second reading of the passage you may wish to share a further thought.

Reflection

Addressing those who gathered with him at Westminster Cathedral for the Papal Mass, the Holy Father reminded us of the need to conform our every thought, word and action to Christ and 'to work strenuously to defend those unchanging moral truths which, taken up, illuminated and confirmed by the Gospel, stand at the foundation of a truly humane, just and free society.' We need to be, he says, 'in the Church and in society, witnesses of the beauty of holiness, witnesses of the splendour of truth, witnesses of the joy and freedom born of a living relationship with Christ!'

In this, Pope Benedict was telling us that happiness and fulfillment are to be found in Christ, just as St Paul addressed the Church in Philippi: 'I regard everything as loss because of the surpassing value of knowing Christ Jesus my Lord. For his sake I have suffered the loss of all things, and I regard them as rubbish, in order that I may gain Christ (Philippians 3:8).' The responsibility for developing this relationship with Christ is ours and cannot be handed over to another. Like Paul we have a chance to 'illuminate' the communities in which we live by living lives characterised by 'holiness'.

Reflecting on all that Pope Benedict said to us in the course of his visit, Archbishop Vincent Nichols has paid particular attention to these words. The beauty of holiness is the holiness of God which can be born in us if we are open to the mystery of God. The splendour of truth is manifested in that ability to proclaim our faith in a gentle and profoundly respectful way such that it is never a battering ram to attack those of other faiths and belief. Joy and happiness are born of a relationship with Christ.

Taking up this theme of joy and happiness, Pope Benedict drew our attention to the crucifix which dominates the nave of Westminster Cathedral. It portrays Christ's body, crushed by suffering, overwhelmed by sorrow, the innocent victim whose death has reconciled us with the Father and given us a share in the very life of God. Whatever failures we have experienced in life, these, as the Holy Father puts it, are 'transformed through the cross'. On the cross, Christ banishes the past to itself. He invites us to live in hope, to be shaped by his forgiveness and love, rather than the mistakes we have made. He carries the cross, the weight of sin and shame, so that we might walk freely. It is this freedom, won for us by the Cross of Christ, rather than our own innocence or cleverness, which lies at the heart of real joy and happiness.

What joy do I find in my faith? How have I shared this with others? What have I done to nourish my relationship with Christ? How have I encouraged others in fulfilling their responsibility to grow in their faith?

Closing Prayers

You may wish to end this session with some different prayers, the Our Father or silent reflection.

Lord, source of eternal life and truth,
give to your shepherd, Pope Benedict,
a spirit of courage, knowledge and love.
By governing with fidelity those entrusted to his care,
may he, as successor to the apostle Peter,
help the Church be a sign of unity, love, and peace.
We ask this through your Son, Jesus Christ,
who lives and reigns with you and the Holy Spirit,
one God, for ever and ever.
Amen.

The full text of Pope Benedict XVI's homily can be found on the Papal Visit website: http://www.thepapalvisit.org.uk/speeches. You may also wish to read section 5 of the Pope's exhortation Verbum Domini where he encourages us to find Christ in the Bible.

 **Notes**

Towards the common good

session six

Opening prayer
Taken from Psalm 143(144)

Leader: Bless the Lord, O my soul.
O Lord, my God, you are very great.
You are clothed with honour and majesty,

Group: You set the earth on its foundations,
so that it shall never be shaken.
You cover it with the deep as with a garment;
the waters stood above the mountains.

Leader: You make springs gush forth in the valleys;
they flow between the hills,
From your lofty abode you water the mountains;
the earth is satisfied with the fruit of your work.

Group: O Lord, how manifold are your works!
In wisdom you have made them all;
the earth is full of your creatures.
When you send forth your spirit, they are created;
and you renew the face of the ground.

Leader: May the glory of the Lord endure for ever;
may the Lord rejoice in his works—
I will sing to the Lord as long as I live;
I will sing praise to my God while I have being.

All: Glory be to the Father, and to the Son and to the Holy Spirit. As it was in the beginning, is now, and ever shall be, world without end. Amen.

For a few moments, either aloud or in the silence of our hearts, let us give thanks to the Lord for all the blessings we have received over the past week. As we give thanks let us remember, again in silence or aloud, all those who need our prayers. Keeping in mind God's mercy, let us remember all the times that we have turned from him and ask for his forgiveness.

Faithful pilgrim

Introduction to Reading of Scripture
Let us listen carefully to the Word of the Lord,
and attend to it with the ear of our hearts.
Let us welcome it, and faithfully put it into practice.

St. Benedict of Nursia (c.480-c.547) adapted

Explore the Scriptures Acts 17:22-31
Then Paul stood in front of the Areopagus and said, 'Athenians, I see how extremely religious you are in every way. For as I went through the city and looked carefully at the objects of your worship, I found among them an altar with the inscription, "To an unknown god." What therefore you worship as unknown, this I proclaim to you. The God who made the world and everything in it, he who is Lord of heaven and earth, does not live in shrines made by human hands, nor is he served by human hands, as though he needed anything, since he himself gives to all mortals life and breath and all things. From one ancestor he made all nations to inhabit the whole earth, and he allotted the times of their existence and the boundaries of the places where they would live, so that they would search for God and perhaps grope for him and find him—though indeed he is not far from each one of us. For "In him we live and move and have our being"; as even some of your own poets have said, "For we too are his offspring."

Since we are God's offspring, we ought not to think that the deity is like gold, or silver, or stone, an image formed by the art and imagination of mortals. While God has overlooked the times of human ignorance, now he commands all people everywhere to repent, because he has fixed a day on which he will have the world judged in righteousness by a man whom he has appointed, and of this he has given assurance to all by raising him from the dead.'

Please take a few moments in silence to reflect on the passage, then share a word or phrase that has struck you. Pause to think about what others have said then after a second reading of the passage you may wish to share a further thought.

Reflection
In the passage above we find St Paul at the Areopagus (which was both a small, rocky hill northwest of the Acropolis in Athens and the venerable council of elders that met in that place). Word had spread to the Athenians of the 'Jesus Way' and so Paul was invited to speak before this council to explain these 'strange ideas'. As we read in Scripture, the response to his impassioned speech was mixed: a few 'sneered', a few asked for more information – perhaps a polite way of saying 'no, thanks' – and a few came to believe (Acts 17:32-33). During his visit, Pope Benedict XVI stood before the great and good of British society in Westminster Hall and

spoke in a way that was, like Paul, not belligerent or aggressive, but which was characterised instead by 'gentleness and respect' (1 Peter 3:15-16).

In his social encyclical *Caritas in veritate*, the Holy Father laid out the need for an ethical underpinning to economic actions. In his address to British society, Pope Benedict went further, asking: 'where is the ethical foundation for political choices to be found?' He explained that the Catholic tradition holds that the basic means for determining what action is 'right' is accessible through reason and not simply though revealed faith. 'According to this understanding,' the Pope said, 'the role of religion in political debate is not so much to supply these norms, as if they could not be known by non-believers – still less to propose concrete political solutions, which would lie altogether outside the competence of religion – but rather to help purify and shed light upon the application of reason to the discovery of objective moral principles.'

'This "corrective" role of religion vis-à-vis reason is not always welcomed, though, partly because distorted forms of religion, such as sectarianism and fundamentalism, can be seen to create serious social problems themselves. And in their turn, these distortions of religion arise when insufficient attention is given to the purifying and structuring role of reason within religion. It is a two-way process. Without the corrective supplied by religion, though, reason too can fall prey to distortions, as when it is manipulated by ideology, or applied in a partial way that fails to take full account of the dignity of the human person. Such misuse of reason, was after all, what gave rise to the slave trade in the first place and to many other social evils, not least the totalitarian ideologies of the twentieth century.'

At our worst, we Christians have isolated and insulated ourselves from our culture's mainstreams. We can be inward-looking, self-absorbed and cloistered,

Westminster Hall

For centuries after its construction in 1097, Westminster Hall acted as the administative and legal centre for the kingdom and it has seen coronation banquets, Oliver Cromwell's inauguration and the trials of King Charles I and St Thomas More. The Pope refered to More's 1535 trial in his address:

'As I speak to you in this historic setting... I recall the figure of Saint Thomas More, the great English scholar and statesman, admired by believers and non-believers alike for the integrity with which he followed his conscience, even at the cost of displeasing the sovereign whose "good servant" he was, because he chose to serve God first.'

instead of engaging with modern society. At our best, we share the truth of God's love through the arts, the spoken word and through social action. This is why Pope Benedict suggests that the world of reason and the world of faith – the world of secular rationality and the world of religious belief – need one another and should not be afraid to enter into a profound and ongoing dialogue, for the good of our civilisation. 'Religion,' His Holiness insisted, 'is not a problem for legislators to solve, but a vital contributor to the national conversation.'

In what kind of society do you want to live? What contemporary attitudes sit uncomfortably with our faith? What do you think faith has to offer society? Am I quiet about my faith - what part does my faith play in my decisions and conversations?

Closing Prayers
You may wish to end this session with some different prayers or silent reflection.

Lord, source of eternal life and truth,
give to your shepherd, Pope Benedict,
a spirit of courage, knowledge and love.
By governing with fidelity those entrusted to his care,
may he, as successor to the apostle Peter,
help the Church be a sign of unity, love, and peace.
We ask this through your Son, Jesus Christ,
who lives and reigns with you and the Holy Spirit,
one God, for ever and ever.
Amen.

The full text of Pope Benedict XVI's address can be found on the Papal Visit website: http://www.thepapalvisit.org.uk/speeches. Some thoughts on the impact of the papal visit by Rabbi Jonathan Sacks and David Cameron MP can be found on p.60

Choosing the common good
Before the Parliamentary elections in 2010, the Bishops' Conference of England & Wales published a document entitled Choosing the Common Good. It echoed an earlier document, The Common Good (1996) which introduced the key themes of Catholic Social Teaching to those who are unfamiliar with them. These documents remind us that the 'common good' refers to what belongs to everyone by virtue of their common humanity; that the dignity of every human life is not our property to dispose of but a gift to treasure. And, that 'where there is no vision, the people perish' (Proverbs 29:18).

Faithful pilgrim

The Holy Father in prayer before the Blessed Sacrament at Hyde Park

Daily Prayer
Sunday to Saturday

The daily prayers on the following pages are drawn from the Divine Office (Liturgy of the Hours). Each day contains a hymn, a Scripture reading, a psalm or Old Testament canticle and a selection of prayers taken from the 'papal feasts': Dedication of the Lateran Basilica (9 Nov), the See of St Peter (22 Feb) and of Saints Peter and Paul (29 June).

Together with the Mass, the Divine Office (Liturgy of the Hours) constitutes the official public prayer life of the Church. It is celebrated, under different names, in both the Eastern and Western Churches. The Divine Office is intended to be read communally but here we invite you to use it as a personal daily prayer.

'The Office is... the prayer not only of the clergy but of the whole People of God.'
Apostolic Constitution, Canticum Laudis

Sunday - A holy temple in the Lord

Introduction
O God, come to our aid. Lord, make haste to help us.

Glory be to the Father and to the Son and to the Holy Spirit, as it was in the beginning, is now, and ever shall be, world without end. Amen. (Alleluia)

omit Alleluias during Lent

Hymn
The Church's one foundation
is Jesus Christ her Lord;
she is his new creation
by water and the Word.
From heaven he came and sought her
to be his holy bride;
with his own blood he bought her,
and for her life he died.

Elect from every nation,
yet one o'er all the earth;
her charter of salvation,
one Lord, one faith, one birth;
one holy name she blesses,
partakes one holy food,
and to one hope she presses,
with every grace endued.

Yet she on earth hath union
with God the Three in One,
and mystic sweet communion
with those whose rest is won.
O happy ones and holy!
Lord, give us grace that we
like them, the meek and lowly,
on high may dwell with thee.

Antiphon
In the temple of the Lord they all cry: 'Glory!'

Psalmody
Canticle 23 (Colossians 1:12-20)

Let us give thanks to the Father,
who has qualified us to share
in the inheritance of the saints in light.

He has delivered us from the dominion of darkness
and transferred us to the kingdom of his beloved Son,
in whom we have redemption,
the forgiveness of sins.

He is the image of the invisible God,
the firstborn of all creation,
for in him all things were created, in heaven and on earth,
visible and invisible.

All things were created through him and for him.
He is before all things,
and in him all things hold together.

He is the head of the body, the Church;
he is the beginning, the firstborn from the dead,
that in everything he might be pre-eminent.

For in him all the fullness of God was pleased to dwell,
and through him to reconcile to himself all things,
whether on earth or in heaven,
making peace by the blood of his cross.

Glory be…

Antiphon
In the temple of the Lord they all cry: 'Glory!'

Reading   Ephesians 2:19-22

You are no longer aliens in a foreign land, but fellow citizens with God's people, members of God's household. You are built upon the foundation laid by the apostles and prophets, and Christ Jesus himself is the foundation stone. In him the whole building is bonded together and grows into a holy temple in the Lord. In him you too are being built with all the rest into a spiritual dwelling for God.

Short Responsory

℟ Your house, Lord, is set apart. It is distinguished by holiness.
℣ As long as time shall last.
Glory be…

Benedictus/Magnificat Antiphon

Glory to you, O Lord, through Christ in the Church

Benedictus (if said in the morning)
or Magnificat (if said in the evening) - see inside front cover for these prayers

Intercessions

Since we are living stones in the temple of Christ's body, let us pray to the Father for his beloved Church and profess our faith in her
℟ This is the house of God and the gate of heaven.
Father cleanse the vineyard of your Church, watch over it and cultivate it with love, until it fills the world and is wonderful to see.
℟ This is the house of God and the gate of heaven.
God of all wisdom, sanctify your house and all the members of your family; let us all see the heavenly city, the new Jerusalem, the bride adorned with glory.
℟ This is the house of God and the gate of heaven.

Our Father…

Concluding prayer

Lord God,
you have called your people to become your Church, grant that all who are gathered in your name may fear you and love you,
may follow you and, under your guidance, attain to your promises in heaven.
We make our prayer through Christ Our Lord.
Amen.

Dedication of the Lateran Basilica

This feast commemorates the dedication of the basilica built by the Emperor Constantine on the Lateran Hill which, by a tradition dating from the twelfth century, is said to have taken place on 9 November.

At first the feast was kept only in the city of Rome but then, in honour of the basilica which is called the Mother and Head of all Churches of the City and the World, it was extended to the whole of the Roman Rite as a sign of unity and respect towards the Holy See, which, as St Ignatius of Antioch wrote, presides over the whole assembly of charity.

Monday - Giving testimony

Introduction
O God, come to our aid. Lord, make haste to help us.

Glory be to the Father and to the Son and to the Holy Spirit, as it was in the beginning, is now, and ever shall be, world without end. Amen. Alleluia.

Hymn
What fairer light is this than time itself doth own,
The golden day with beams more radiant brightening?
The princes of God's church this feast-day doth enthrone,
To sinners heavenward bound their burden lightening.

One taught mankind its creed, one guards the heavenly gate.
Founders of Rome, they bind the world in loyalty;
One by the sword achieved, one by the cross his fate;
With laurelled brows they hold eternal royalty.

Rejoice, O Rome, this day; thy walls they once did sign
With princely blood, who now their glory share with thee.
What city's vesture glows with crimson deep as thine?
What beauty else has earth that may compare with thee?

Antiphon
I have prayed for you, Peter, that your faith may not fail, and when you have repented, you must strengthen your brothers.

Psalmody
Psalm 96 (97)

The Lord is king, let earth rejoice,
let all the coastlands be glad.
Cloud and darkness are his raiment;
his throne, justice and right.

A fire prepares his path;
it burns up his foes on every side.
His lightnings light up the world,
the earth trembles at the sight.

The mountains melt like wax
before the Lord of all the earth.
The skies proclaim his justice;
all peoples see his glory.

The Lord loves those who hate evil;
he guards the souls of his saints;
he sets them free from the wicked.

Light shines forth for the just
and joy for the upright of heart.
Rejoice, you just, in the Lord;
give glory to his holy name.

Glory be…

Antiphon
I have prayed for you, Peter, that your faith may not fail, and when you have repented, you must strengthen your brothers.

Reading
1 Corinthians 15:3-5,8

In the first place, I taught you what I had been taught myself, namely that Christ died for our sins, in accordance with the scriptures; that he was buried, and that he was raised to life on the third day, in accordance with the scriptures; that he appeared first to Cephas and secondly to the Twelve and last of all he appeared to me too.

Short Responsory
℟ The apostles proclaimed the word of God and feared no one.
℣ They gave testimony to the resurrection of Jesus Christ.
Glory be…

Benedictus/Magnificat Antiphon
Peter the apostle and Paul the teacher of the nations taught us your law, Lord.

Benedictus (if said in the morning) or Magnificat (if said in the evening) - see inside front cover for these prayers

Intercessions
We pray to Christ who built his Church on the foundation of the apostles and prophets.
℟ Lord, be with your people.
When the disciples feared that the ship was sinking, you commanded the sea and there was calm: protect your Church in the midst of trouble, and give her the peace that the world cannot give.
℟ Lord, be with your people.
After your resurrection you gathered your Church around Peter: gather all your people now into the unity for which you prayed
℟ Lord, be with your people.

Our Father…

Concluding prayer
Almighty, ever-living God,
you give us the great joy of honouring the apostles Peter and Paul.
Grant that your Church
may follow their teaching to the full,
because these are the men
who first taught us to worship you in Christ, your Son,
who lives and reigns with you and the Holy Spirit,
God, for ever and ever.
Amen.

El Greco's *Apostles Peter and Paul* (1587-92)

Tuesday - A firm foundation

Introduction
O God, come to our aid. Lord, make haste to help us.

Glory be to the Father and to the Son and to the Holy Spirit, as it was in the beginning, is now, and ever shall be, world without end. Amen. Alleluia.

Hymn
O Peter, who were named by Christ
The guardian-shepherd of his flock,
Protect the Church he built on you
To stand unyielding, firm on rock.

Your weakness Christ exchanged strength,
You faltered, but he made you true;
He knew the greatness of your love
And gave the keys of heaven to you.

Unseen, eternal Trinity,
We give you glory, praise your name;
Your love keeps faith with faithless men,
Through change and stress you are the same.

Antiphon
The Lord said to Simon, 'Do not fear, from now on you will be a fisher of men.'

Psalmody
Psalm 62 (63)

O God, you are my God, for you I long;
for you my soul is thirsting.
My body pines for you
like a dry, weary land without water.
So I gaze on you in the sanctuary
to see your strength and your glory.

For your love is better than life,
my lips will speak your praise.
So I will bless you all my life,
in your name I will lift up my hands.
My soul shall be filled as with a banquet,
my mouth shall praise you with joy.

On my bed I remember you.
On you I muse through the night
for you have been my help;
in the shadow of your wings I rejoice.
My soul clings to you;
your right hand holds me fast.

Glory be…

Antiphon
The Lord said to Simon, 'Do not fear, from now on you will be a fisher of men.'

Reading
2 Peter 1:16

It was not any cleverly invented myths that we were repeating when we brought you the knowledge of the power and the coming of our Lord Jesus Christ; we had seen his majesty for ourselves.

Short Responsory
℟ You will make them rulers over all the land.
℣ Your name, Lord, will be remembered.
Glory be…

Benedictus/Magnificat Antiphon
Peter said: God raised up and glorified Jesus, whom you had put to death.

Benedictus (if said in the morning) or Magnificat (if said in the evening) - see inside front cover for these prayers

Intercessions

Since we have received from the apostles our heavenly inheritance, let us thank our Father for all his blessings.
℟ Lord, the apostles sing your praises.

Praise to you, Lord God, for the gift of Christ's body and blood, handed on by the apostles, to give us strength and life.
℟ Lord, the apostles sing your praises.

For the table of the word, served by the apostles, to bring us light and joy.
℟ Lord, the apostles sing your praises.

For your holy Church, built on the apostles, to make us all one body.
℟ Lord, the apostles sing your praises.

Our Father…

Concluding prayer

Almighty God,
as you built your Church
on the rock of Peter's faith,
grant that with such a firm foundation
we may hold fast in every storm.
We make our prayer through
Christ our Lord.
Amen.

The See of Saint Peter the Apostle

The feast of the See of St Peter has been kept at Rome on the 22 February from the fourth century as a symbol of the unity of the Church founded on the Apostle St Peter, the rock on which Christ has built his Church (Matthew 16:18).

Wednesday - Following Christ

Introduction
O God, come to our aid. Lord, make haste to help us.

Glory be to the Father and to the Son and to the Holy Spirit, as it was in the beginning, is now, and ever shall be, world without end. Amen. Alleluia.

Hymn
What fairer light is this than time itself doth own,
The golden day with beams more radiant brightening?
The princes of God's church this feast-day doth enthrone,
To sinners heavenward bound their burden lightening.

One taught mankind its creed, one guards the heavenly gate.
Founders of Rome, they bind the world in loyalty;
One by the sword achieved, one by the cross his fate;
With laurelled brows they hold eternal royalty.

Rejoice, O Rome, this day; thy walls they once did sign
With princely blood, who now their glory share with thee.
What city's vesture glows with crimson deep as thine?
What beauty else has earth that may compare with thee?

Antiphon
Go, preach the Good News of the kingdom: you received without cost; give without charge.

Psalmody
Psalm 127(128)
O blessed are those who fear the Lord and walk in his ways!

By the labour of your hands you shall eat.
You will be happy and prosper;
Your wife like a fruitful vine
in the heart of your house;
Your children like shoots of the olive,
around your table.

Indeed thus shall be blessed
the man who fears the Lord.
May the Lord bless you from Zion
all the days of your life!
May you see your children's children
in a happy Jerusalem!

On Israel, peace!

Antiphon
Go, preach the Good News of the kingdom: you received without cost; give without charge.

Reading
2 Corinthians 4:13
Scripture says: 'I spoke because I believed.' In the same spirit of faith, we also speak because we believe. For we know that God who raised the Lord Jesus to life will also raise us up with Jesus and bring us together with you in his presence.

Short responsory
℟ All will know that you are my disciples.
℣ If there is love among you.

Glory be…

Benedictus/Magnificat Antiphon

The holy city of Jerusalem had twelve foundation-stones, and on them were the names of the twelve apostles of the Lamb. The Lamb himself was the light of the city.

Benedictus (if said in the morning) or Magnificat (if said in the evening) - see inside front cover for these prayers

Intercessions

We pray to Christ who built his Church on the foundation of the apostles and prophets.
℟ Lord, be with your people.
Simon the fisherman was called by you to be a fisher of men: call others today to share in this task.
℟ Lord, be with your people.
You sent Paul as an apostle to all: let your good news be preached today through all creation.
℟ Lord, be with your people.
You entrusted the keys of the kingdom to your Church: open the gates of life to the dead who put their trust in you.
℟ Lord, be with your people.

Our Father…

Concluding prayer

Lord our God,
may the blessed apostles Peter and Paul support us by their prayers.
Though them you first taught your Church the Christian faith.
Provide us now, by their intercession, with help for our eternal salvation.
We make our prayer through Christ our Lord.
Amen.

The Feast of Saints Peter and Paul

The Feast of Saints Peter and Paul, celebrated on 29 June, is a liturgical feast in honour of the martyrdom in Rome of the apostles Saint Peter and Saint Paul and is a holy day of obligation in England and Wales. The celebration is of ancient origin, the date selected being the anniversary either of their death or of the translation of their relics. On this day the Roman Church celebrates, too, the anniversary of Pope Benedict XVI's election (19 April 2005) and newly created metropolitan archbishops receive their pallium (for more on the pallium and the papal fisherman's ring see pp.54-55).

Thursday - Showing us the Kingdom

Introduction
O God, come to our aid. Lord, make haste to help us.

Glory be to the Father and to the Son and to the Holy Spirit, as it was in the beginning, is now, and ever shall be, world without end. Amen. Alleluia.

Hymn
Jesus, true God and Rock of our salvation!
Yours is the title that you gave to Simon,
Naming him Peter as the Church's bedrock,
First of apostles!

Jesus, sole Ruler in the Church, your kingdom,
Yours are the keys that open David's city!
Yet till your coming Peter is your viceroy,
Keys in his keeping!

Jesus, we thank you for the Church, your Body!
Keep us all one with you and with each other,
One with our bishop, one with your chief shepherd,
Peter's successor!

Antiphon
While Peter was held in prison the Church prayed unceasingly to God for him.

Psalmody
Psalm 125(126)

When the Lord delivered Zion from bondage,
it seemed like a dream.
Then was our mouth filled with laughter,
on our lips there were songs.

The heathens themselves said: 'What marvels
the Lord worked for them!'
What marvels the Lord worked for us!
Indeed we were glad.

Deliver us, O Lord, from our bondage
as streams in dry land.
Those who are sowing in tears
will sing when they reap.

They go out, they go out, full of tears,
carrying seed for the sowing:
they come back, they come back, full of song,
carrying their sheaves.

Antiphon
While Peter was held in prison the Church prayed unceasingly to God for him.

Reading
1 Peter 1:3-5

Blessed be God the Father of our Lord Jesus Christ, who in his great mercy has given us a new birth as his children, by raising Jesus Christ from the dead, so that we have a sure hope and the promise of an inheritance that can never be spoilt or soiled and never fade away, because it is being kept for you in the heavens. Through your faith, God's power will guard you until the salvation which has been prepared is revealed at the end of time.

Short Responsory
℟ Tell of the glory of the Lord; announce it among the nations.
℣ Speak of his wonderful deeds to all the peoples.
Glory be…

Benedictus/Magnificat Antiphon
You are the shepherd of the flock, the prince of the apostles: to you were given the keys of the kingdom of heaven.

Benedictus (if said in the morning) or Magnificat (if said in the evening) - see inside front cover for these prayers

Intercessions
Father, when your son rose from the dead, you showed him first to the apostles; let us make him known, near and far
℟ Lord, remember your Church.
You sent your Son into the world to proclaim the good news to the poor; grant that we may bring his gospel into the darkness.
℟ Lord, remember your Church.
You sent your Son to reconcile the world to yourself by the shedding of his blood; let us become his fellow workers in restoring men to your friendship.
℟ Lord, remember your Church.
You sent your Son to plant in the hearts of all the seed of imperishable life; may we labour to sow his word and reap a harvest of joy.
℟ Lord, remember your Church.

Our Father...

Concluding prayer
Almighty God,
as you built your Church
on the rock of Peter's faith,
grant that with such a firm foundation
we may hold fast in every storm.
We make our prayer through
Christ our Lord.
Amen.

Detail from Fra Angelico's *Last Judgement* (1425-30)

Friday - On earth as it is in heaven

Introduction
O God, come to our aid. Lord, make haste to help us.

Glory be to the Father and to the Son and to the Holy Spirit, as it was in the beginning, is now, and ever shall be, world without end. Amen. Alleluia.

Hymn
O fathers of our ancient faith,
with all the heav'ns we sing your fame
Whose sound went forth in all the earth
To tell of Christ, and bless his name.

You took the gospel to the poor,
The word of God alight in you,
Which in our day is told again:
That timeless word, for ever new.

You told of God who died for us
And out of death triumphant rose,
who gave the truth that made us free,
And changeless through the ages goes.

Praise Father, Son and Holy Ghost
Whose gift is faith that never dies:
A light in darkness now, until
The day-star in our hearts arise.

Stanbrook Abbey Hymnal

Antiphon
I know who it is that I have put my trust in, and I am certain that he, the just judge, will be able to take care of all I have entrusted to me until that Day.

Psalmody
Canticle 21 (Ephesians 1:3-10)

Blest be the God and Father
of our Lord Jesus Christ,
who has blessed us in Christ
with every spiritual blessing
in the heavenly places.

He chose us in him
before the foundation of the world,
that we should be holy
and blameless before him.

He destined us in love
to be his sons through Jesus Christ,
according to the purpose of his will,
to the praise of his glorious grace
which he freely bestowed on us in the Beloved.

In him we have redemption through his blood,
the forgiveness of our trespasses,
according to the riches of his grace
which he lavished upon us.

He has made known to us
in all wisdom and insight
the mystery of his will,
according to his purpose
that he set forth in Christ.

His purpose he set forth in Christ
as a plan for the fullness of time,
to unite all things in him,
things in heaven and things on earth.

Antiphon
I know who it is that I have put my trust in, and I am certain that he, the just judge, will be able to take care of all I have entrusted to me until that Day.

Reading
Acts 15:7-9

God chose me from among you to preach the message of Good News to the Gentiles, so that they could hear and believe. And God, who knows the hearts of men, showed his approval of the Gentiles by giving the gift of the Holy Spirit to them just as he had to us. He made no difference between us and them; he forgave them their sins because they believed.

Short Responsory
℟ Praise the Lord, all you nations, acclaim him all you peoples.
℣ Strong is his love for us, he is faithful forever.
Glory be…

Benedictus/Magnificat Antiphon
Glorious are the apostles of Christ; they loved each other in this life; they are not separated in death.

Benedictus (if said in the morning) or Magnificat (if said in the evening) - see inside front cover for these prayers

Intercessions
We pray to Christ who built his Church on the rock, and sent his apostles as witnesses to his victory over death.
℟ Lord, remember your Church.
When you had risen from the dead you appeared to Peter and revealed yourself to Paul: help us to live in the power of your resurrection
℟ Lord, remember your Church.
Heavenly Father, you placed your Son at your own right hand in heaven; receive the dead into the happiness of your kingdom.
℟ Lord, remember your Church.

Our Father…

Concluding prayer
Almighty, ever-living God,
you give us the great joy of honouring the apostles Peter and Paul.
Grant that your Church
may follow their teaching to the full,
because these are the men
who first taught us to worship you in Christ, your Son,
who lives and reigns with you and the Holy Spirit,
God, for ever and ever.
Amen.

Detail from Gian Lorenzo Bernini's *Cathedra Petri* (1647-53) in St Peter's basilica, Rome

Saturday - For the sake of his name

Introduction
O God, come to our aid. Lord, make haste to help us.

Glory be to the Father and to the Son and to the Holy Spirit, as it was in the beginning, is now, and ever shall be, world without end. Amen. Alleluia.

Hymn
Let all on earth their voices raise,
Re-echoing heav'ns triumphant praise,
To him who gave th' apostles grace
To run on earth their glorious race.

Thou at whose word they bore the light
Of gospel truth o'er heathen night,
To us that heavenly light impart,
to glad our eyes and cheer our heart.

Thou at whose will to them was given
To bind and loose in earth and heaven,
Our chains unbind, our sins undo,
And in our hearts thy grace renew.

Thou in whose might they spoke the word
Which cured disease and health restored,
To us its healing power prolong,
Support the weak, confirm the strong.
Tr R. Mant 1776-1848

Antiphon
The grace of God in me has not been fruitless; rather his grace remains with me always.

Psalmody
Psalm 18(19)

The heavens proclaim the glory of God,
and the firmament shows forth the work of his hands.
Day unto day takes up the story
and night unto night makes known the message.

No speech, no word, no voice is heard
yet their span extends through all the earth,
their words to the utmost bounds of the world.

There he has placed a tent for the sun;
it comes forth like a bridegroom coming from his tent,
rejoices like a champion to run its course.

At the end of the sky is the rising of the sun;
to the furthest end of the sky is its course.
There is nothing concealed from its burning heat.

Antiphon
The grace of God in me has not been fruitless; rather his grace remains with me always.

Reading
Hebrews 13:12-13

My dear people, if you can have some share in the sufferings of Christ, be glad, because you will enjoy a much greater gladness when his glory is revealed. It is a blessing for you when they insult you for bearing the name of Christ, because it means that you have the spirit of glory, the spirit of God resting on you.

Short responsory
℟ They lay down their lives for the sake of our Lord Jesus Christ.
℣ They went away rejoicing that they had had the honour of suffering humiliation.
Glory be…

Benedictus/Magnificat Antiphon
Simon Peter said, 'Lord, to whom shall we go? You have the words of eternal life; we believe and we know that you are Christ, the Son of God.

Benedictus (if said in the morning) or Magnificat (if said in the evening) - see inside front cover for these prayers

Intercessions
We pray to Christ who built his Church on the rock, and sent his apostles as witnesses to his victory over death:
℟ Lord, be with your Church.
You prayed that the faith of Peter might not fail: strengthen and sustain the faith of your Church
℟ Lord, be with your Church.
Peter denied you, but your love drew him back to you: whatever we have done in the past, keep us close to your merciful love.
℟ Lord, be with your Church.

Our Father…

Concluding prayer
Lord our God,
may the blessed apostles Peter and Paul support us by their prayers.
Though them you first taught your Church the Christian faith.
Provide us now, by their intercession, with help for our eternal salvation.
We make our prayer through Christ our Lord.
Amen.

Saints Peter and Paul by Irina Bradley

Supplementary resources

- Quotes from the visit
- An introduction to Papal documents since 2005
- Papal symbols and the coat of arms
- Apostolic succession - from Peter to Benedict XVI
- Reactions to the papal visit
- Other resources

Quotes from Pope Benedict XVI's visit to the United Kingdom (16-19 September 2010)

Proclaim the Gospel
'At the same time, we Christians must never hesitate to proclaim our faith in the uniqueness of the salvation won for us by Christ.'

Pope Benedict XVI, Address at Lambeth Palace, 17th Sept. 2010

'…the urgent need to proclaim the Gospel afresh in a highly secularised environment. In the course of my visit it has become clear to me how deep a thirst there is among the British people for the Good News of Jesus Christ. You have been chosen by God to offer them the living water of the Gospel, encouraging them to place their hopes, not in the vain enticements of this world, but in the firm assurances of the next. As you proclaim the coming of the Kingdom, with its promise of hope for the poor and the needy, the sick and the elderly, the unborn and the neglected, be sure to present in its fullness the life-giving message of the Gospel, including those elements which call into question the widespread assumptions of today's culture. As you know, a Pontifical Council has recently been established for the New Evangelisation of countries of long-standing Christian tradition, and I would encourage you to avail yourselves of its services in addressing the task before you. Moreover, many of the new ecclesial movements have a particular charism for evangelisation, and I know that you will continue to explore appropriate and effective ways of involving them in the mission of the Church.'

Pope Benedict XVI, Address at Oscott, 19 September 2010

'The evangelisation of culture is all the more important in our times, when a "dictatorship of relativism" threatens to obscure the unchanging truth about man's nature, his destiny and his ultimate good.'

Homily at Bellahouston, 16 September 2010

'Today's Gospel reminds us that Christ continues to send his disciples into the world in order to proclaim the coming of his Kingdom and to bring his peace into the world, beginning house by house, family by family, town by town.'

Homily at Bellahouston, 16 September 2010

'…the Church cannot withdraw from the task of proclaiming Christ and his Gospel as saving truth, the source of our ultimate happiness as individuals and as the foundation of a just and humane society.'

Reflection at Hyde Park, 18 September 2010

Essential Role of the Laity in Mission

'The Second Vatican Council spoke eloquently of the indispensable role of the laity in carrying forward the Church's mission through their efforts to serve as a leaven of the Gospel in society and to work for the advancement of God's Kingdom in the world (cf. Lumen Gentium, 31; Apostolicam Actuositatem, 7). The Council's appeal to the lay faithful to take up their baptismal sharing in Christ's mission echoed the insights and teachings of John Henry Newman. May the profound ideas of this great Englishman continue to inspire all Christ's followers in this land to conform their every thought, word and action to Christ, and to work strenuously to defend those unchanging moral truths which, taken up, illuminated and confirmed by the Gospel, stand at the foundation of a truly humane, just and free society.'

Homily at Westminster Cathedral, 18 September 2010

'One of the Cardinal's best-loved meditations includes the words, "God has created me to do him some definite service. He has committed some work to me which he has not committed to another" (Meditations on Christian Doctrine). Here we see Newman's fine Christian realism, the point at which faith and life inevitably intersect. Faith is meant to bear fruit in the transformation of our world through the power of the Holy Spirit at work in the lives and activity of believers… But each of us, in accordance with his or her state of life, is called to work for the advancement of God's Kingdom by imbuing temporal life with the values of the Gospel. Each of us has a mission, each of us is called to change the world, to work for a culture of life, a culture forged by love and respect for the dignity of each human person. As our Lord tells us in the Gospel we have just heard, our light must shine in the sight of all, so that, seeing our good works, they may give praise to our heavenly Father (cf. Mt 5:16).'

Reflection at Hyde Park, 18 September 2010

'Newman helps us to understand what this means for our daily lives: he tells us that our divine Master has assigned a specific task to each one of us, a "definite service", committed uniquely to every single person: "I have my mission", he wrote, "I am a link in a chain, a bond of connection between persons. He has not created me for naught. I shall do good, I shall do his work; I shall be an angel of peace, a preacher of truth in my own place … if I do but keep his commandments and serve him in my calling" (Meditations and Devotions, 301-2).'

Homily at Cofton Park, 19 September 2010

'The definite service to which Blessed John Henry was called involved applying his keen intellect and his prolific pen to many of the most pressing "subjects of the day".'

Homily at Cofton Park, 19 September 2010

Call to Holiness and Transparency

'…the Church does not seek to be attractive in and of herself, but must be transparent for Jesus Christ and to the extent that she is not out for herself, as a strong and powerful body in the world, that wants power, but is simply the voice of another, she becomes truly transparent for the great figure of Christ and the great truth that he has brought to humanity. The power of love, in this moment one listens, one accepts. The Church should not consider herself, but help to consider the other and she herself must see and speak of the other.'

In flight interview, 16 September 2010

'I hope that among those of you listening to me today there are some of the future saints of the twenty-first century. What God wants most of all for each one of you is that you should become holy. He loves you much more than you could ever begin to imagine, and he wants the very best for you. And by far the best thing for you is to grow in holiness.'

Address at the Big Assembly, 17 September 2010

'...we shall be effective defenders or proclaimers of our faith when we can show what a holy life looks like, a life in which the joy of God is transparently present.'

Archbishop Rowan Williams at Lambeth Palace, 17 September 2010

'We pray that our hearts will be ever more open to the presence and power of the Holy Spirit so that our lives may radiate the Light of Christ to those around us.'

Archbishop Peter Smith, Welcome at Hyde Park, 18 September 2010

Examples for us to follow

'…the Church of the apostles, the Church of the martyrs, the Church of the saints, the Church which Newman loved and to whose mission he devoted his entire life.'

Pope Benedict XVI, Reflection at Hyde Park, 18 September 2010

'This nation, and the Europe which Bede and his contemporaries helped to build, once again stands at the threshold of a new age. May Saint Bede's example inspire the Christians of these lands…'

Address at Westminster Abbey, 17 September 2010

These quotes were taken from materials produced by the Home Mission Desk at the Bishops' Conference of England & Wales and are used with permission. Further resources building on the legacy of the historic papal visit can be found on their website - http://www.thepapalvisit.org.uk

Selected writings of Pope Benedict XVI

Papal encyclicals

Deus caritas est (God is Love) - 25 December 2005
In today's high-tech, fast-paced world, love is often portrayed as being separate from Church teaching. With his first encyclical, Pope Benedict XVI hopes to overturn that perception and describe the essential place of love in the life of the Church. The Holy Father explains the various dimensions of love, highlighting the distinctions between 'eros' and 'agape,' Jesus as the incarnate love of God, and the scriptural law of love. In part two, he links the Church's charitable work with the love of God as Trinity, noting that the Church must express love through acts of justice and charity. This encyclical is an ideal reflection for religious and civic leaders, those preparing for marriage, and those engaged in justice and charitable work.

Spe Salvi (In hope we are saved) - 30 November 2007
In his encyclical letter On Christian Hope, Pope Benedict XVI elaborates the significance of Christian hope in eternal life for contemporary Catholics by presenting examples of hope from the New Testament and saints of the Church. After affirming the modern practice of working to progress in faith with the help of reason, he reminds readers that hope ultimately depends on trusting in God's love for us, and that Christians can be strengthened by turning to God together, in community.

Caritas in Veritate (Charity in Truth) - 29 June 2009
Pope Benedict's third encyclical, *Caritas in Veritate*, is a call to see the relationship between human and environmental ecologies and to link charity and truth in the pursuit of justice, the common good, and authentic human development. In doing so, the pope points out the responsibilities and limitations of government and the private market, challenges traditional ideologies of right and left, and calls all men and women to think and act anew.

All of these documents can be viewed on the Vatican website and are listed under Papal Archive - http://www.vatican.va/holy_father/benedict_xvi/index.htm

Apostolic Exhortations

Sacramentum Caritatis (Sacrament of Love) - 22 February 2007
Set alongside Pope Benedict XVI's first encyclical God Is Love (*Deus Caritas Est*) where he stressed the relationship between the Eucharist and love, The Sacrament of Love (or Charity) picks up that theme and expands it as Pope Benedict explores the mystery of eucharistic faith and how it reveals the mystery of the Trinity. Released on the Feast of the Seat of St. Peter, the Holy Father examines the important relationship between the Eucharist and the other sacraments, including the sacrament of the Church. He also highlights the social implications of the Eucharist and firmly connects it with the Church's social teaching.

Verbum Domini (The Word of the Lord) - 30 September 2010
Following on from the 2008 Synod of Bishops devoted to 'The Word of God in the Life and the Mission of the Church,' *Verbum Domini* has been billed as the most important Church document on Scripture since *Dei Verbum*, Vatican II's Dogmatic Constitution on Divine Revelation (1965). Its purpose is to communicate the results of the Synod; rediscover the Word of God – a source of constant ecclesial renewal; to promote the Bible among pastors; to help the faithful become witnesses of the Word of God; to support the new evangelisation and ecumenical dialogue; and to foster ever greater love for the Word of God.

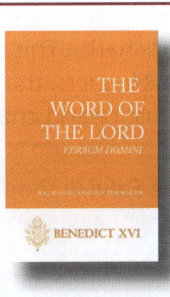

Other letters, messages and addresses

Ubicumque et semper - 21 September 2010
Apostolic Letter (Motu Proprio data) establishing the Pontifical Council for Promoting the New Evangelisation. [http://www.zenit.org/article-30619?l=english]

Anglicanorum coetibus - 4 November 2009
Apostolic Constitution providing for Personal Ordinariates for Anglicans entering into Full Communion with the Catholic Church. [http://www.zenit.org/article-27490?l=english]

Angelus - Regina Coeli - each Sunday at noon
The Holy Father gives a short homily on the day. Videos available on vatican.va.

General Audience - each Wednesday
The Holy Father gives a catechesis on a theme, recently the Pope has chosen to reflect on the lives of the saints. Videos available from the Vatican website.

Papal symbols

During his inauguration homily on 24 April 2005, Pope Benedict XVI spoke of two symbols which reflect his ministry as the successor of St Peter: the pallium (a woollen band worn around the neck) and the ring of the fisherman.

The Pallium

'The first symbol is the Pallium, woven in pure wool, which will be placed on my shoulders. This ancient sign, which the Bishops of Rome have worn since the fourth century, may be considered an image of the yoke of Christ. God's yoke is God's will, which we accept. It does not weigh down on us, oppressing us and taking away our freedom. To know what God wants, to know where the path of life is found – this was Israel's joy, this was her great privilege. It is also our joy… The symbolism of the Pallium is even more concrete: the lamb's wool is meant to represent the lost, sick or weak sheep which the shepherd places on his shoulders and carries to the waters of life. The human race – every one of us – is the sheep lost in the desert which no longer knows the way. The Son of God will not let this happen; he cannot abandon humanity in so wretched a condition. He leaps to his feet and abandons the glory of heaven, in order to go in search of the sheep and pursue it, all the way to the Cross. He is the good shepherd who lays down his life for the sheep.

'What the Pallium indicates first and foremost is that we are all carried by Christ. But at the same time it invites us to carry one another. Hence the Pallium becomes a symbol of the shepherd's mission. The pastor must be inspired by Christ's holy zeal: for him it is not a matter of indifference that so many people are living in the desert. And there are so many kinds of desert. There is the desert of poverty, the desert of hunger and thirst, the desert of abandonment, of loneliness, of destroyed love. There is the desert of God's darkness, the emptiness of souls no longer aware of their dignity or the goal of human life… The Church as a whole and all her Pastors, like Christ, must set out to lead people out of the desert, towards the place of life, towards friendship with the Son of God, towards the One who gives us life, and life in abundance.

'The symbol of the lamb also has a deeper meaning. In the Ancient Near East, it was customary for kings to style themselves shepherds of their people… to them their subjects were like sheep, which the shepherd could dispose of as he wished.

'When the shepherd of all humanity, living God, himself became a lamb, he stood on the side of the lambs, with those who are downtrodden and killed. It is not power, but love that redeems us!

'"Feed my sheep", says Christ to Peter, and now, at this moment, he says it to me as well… My dear friends – at this moment I can only say: pray for me, that I may learn to love the Lord more and more. Pray for me, that I may learn to love each one of you and all of you together. Pray for me, that I may not flee for fear of the wolves. Let us pray for one another, that the Lord will carry us and that we will learn to carry one another.'

The Fisherman's Ring

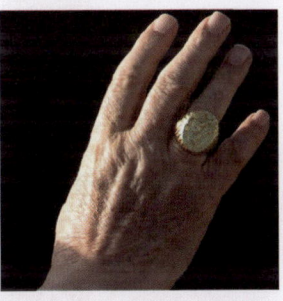

'The second symbol used in today's liturgy to express the inauguration of the Petrine Ministry is the presentation of the fisherman's ring. Peter's call to be a shepherd, which we heard in the Gospel, comes after the account of a miraculous catch of fish: after a night in which the disciples had let down their nets without success, they see the Risen Lord on the shore. He tells them to let down their nets once more, and the nets become so full that they can hardly pull them in; 153 large fish: "and although there were so many, the net was not torn" (John 21:11)… The Church and the successors of the Apostles are told to put out into the deep sea of history and to let down the nets, so as to win men and women over to the Gospel – to God, to Christ, to true life.

'A fish is created for water, it is fatal to be taken out of the sea, to be removed from its vital element to serve as human food. But in the mission of a fisher of men, the reverse is true. We are living in alienation, in the salt waters of suffering and death; in a sea of darkness without light. The net of the Gospel pulls us out of the waters of death and brings us into the splendour of God's light, into true life… The purpose of our lives is to reveal God to others. Only when we meet the living God in Christ do we know what life is. We are not some casual and meaningless product of evolution. Each of us is the result of a thought of God. Each of us is willed, each of us is loved, each of us is necessary. There is nothing more beautiful than to be surprised by the Gospel, by the encounter with Christ. There is nothing more beautiful than to know Him and to speak to others of our friendship with Him. The task of the shepherd, the task of the fisher of men, can often seem wearisome. But it is beautiful and wonderful, because it is truly a service to joy, to God's joy which longs to break into the world.'

Pope Benedict XVI's coat of arms

The coat of arms of Pope Benedict XVI incorporates both papal elements, as well as the elements of the coat of arms he bore as Archbishop of München (Munich) and Freising, and as the Prefect of the Congregation for the Doctrine of the Faith.

Mitre

The mitre replaces the 'beehive' tiara from former papal coats of arms. Pope Paul VI dropped the ceremonial use of the tiara although he as well as John Paul I and John Paul II retained it in their coats of arms. Benedict XVI has replaced it with the mitre, on which are three gold bands representing 'order, jurisdiction and magisterium.' These are the symbolic equivalents of the three layers of the tiara. They are connected by the vertical gold strip, representing the unity of these three kinds of authority in the person of the Supreme Pontiff.

Pallium

The use of the white pallium with red crosses draped below the shield is a new addition to papal coats of arms. It represents episcopal authority, the special kind of jurisdiction that is reserved to metropolitan archbishops in their province and to the pope universally in the Church.

Crossed Keys

The two crossed keys symbolise the powers Christ gave to the Apostle Peter and to his successors. 'I will give you the keys to the kingdom of heaven.' (Matthew 16:19) The gold key represents the power to bind in heaven and the silver key spiritual authority on earth. The two keys are united by the cord, again indicating their essential unity in Peter and his successors.

Caput Aethiopum

The shield displays the 'Moor of Freising.' The Moor's head, facing left and typically crowned, appeared on the coat of arms of the old principality of Freising as early as 1316. Ever since 1802-1803 the archbishops of Munich and Freising have included the Caput Aethiopum, the head of an Ethiopian, in their episcopal coat of arms.

Bear of Corbinian

The saintly Bishop Corbinian preached the Christian faith in the Duchy of Bavaria in the 8th century and is considered the spiritual father and patron of the archdiocese. A legend states that he travelled to Rome with a bear as his pack-animal. He released the bear on arrival and it returned to Bavaria. It symbolises the burden of office.

Scallop Shell

The shell has many meanings. St Augustine was once walking along the seashore, meditating on the mystery of the Holy Trinity when he saw a boy using a shell to pour seawater into a little hole. When Augustine asked him what he was doing, he replied, 'I am emptying the sea into this hole.' Augustine then understood that depths of the mystery of God were inpenetrable. The shell also symbolises pilgrimage. In Church art it is a symbol of the apostle James the Great and his sanctuary at Santiago de Compostela in Spain. This symbol also alludes to 'the pilgrim people of God,' a title for the Church which Fr Joseph Ratzinger championed at Vatican II.

From St Peter to Benedict XVI

St Peter (32-67)
St Linus (67-76)
St Anacletus (Cletus) (76-88)
St Clement I (88-97)
St Evaristus (97-105)
St Alexander I (105-115)
St Sixtus I (115-125)
St Telesphorus (125-136)
St Hyginus (136-140)
St Pius I (140-155)
St Anicetus (155-166)
St Soter (166-175)
St Eleutherius (175-189)
St Victor I (189-199)
St Zephyrinus (199-217)
St Callistus I (217-22)
St Urban I (222-30)
St Pontain (230-35)
St Anterus (235-36)
St Fabian (236-50)
St Cornelius (251-53)
St Lucius I (253-54)
St Stephen I (254-257)
St Sixtus II (257-258)
St Dionysius (260-268)
St Felix I (269-274)
St Eutychian (275-283)
St Caius (283-296)
St Marcellinus (296-304)
St Marcellus I (308-309)
St Eusebius (309 or 310)
St Miltiades (311-14)
St Sylvester I (314-35)
St Marcus (336)
St Julius I (337-52)
Liberius (352-66)
St Damasus I (366-83)
St Siricius (384-99)
St Anastasius I (399-401)
St Innocent I (401-17)
St Zosimus (417-18)
St Boniface I (418-22)
St Celestine I (422-32)
St Sixtus III (432-40)
St Leo I (the Great) (440-61)
St Hilarius (461-68)

St Simplicius (468-83)
St Felix III (II) (483-92)
St Gelasius I (492-96)
Anastasius II (496-98)
St Symmachus (498-514)
St Hormisdas (514-23)
St John I (523-26)
St Felix IV (III) (526-30)
Boniface II (530-32)
St Agapetus I (535-36)
St Silverius (536-37)
Vigilius (537-55)
Pelagius I (556-61)
John III (561-74)
Benedict I (575-79)
Pelagius II (579-90)

St Gregory I (Great) (590-604) sent St Augustine to England in 597 to convert the country to Christianity

Sabinian (604-606)
Boniface III (607)
St Boniface IV (608-15)
St Deusdedit (Adeodatus I) (615-18)
Boniface V (619-25)
Honorius I (625-38)
Severinus (640)
John IV (640-42)
Theodore I (642-49)
St Martin I (649-55)
St Eugene I (655-57)
St Vitalian (657-72)
Adeodatus (II) (672-76)
Donus (676-78)
St Agatho (678-81)
St Leo II (682-83)
St Benedict II (684-85)
John V (685-86)
Conon (686-87)
St Sergius I (687-701)
John VI (701-05)
John VII (705-07)
Sisinnius (708)

Constantine (708-15)
St Gregory II (715-31)
St Gregory III (731-41)
St Zachary (741-52)
Stephen II (752)
Stephen III (752-57)
St Paul I (757-67)
Stephen IV (767-72)
Adrian I (772-95)
St Leo III (795-816)
Stephen V (816-17)
St Paschal I (817-24)
Eugene II (824-27)
Valentine (827)
Gregory IV (827-44)
Sergius II (844-47)
St Leo IV (847-55)
Benedict III (855-58)
St Nicholas I (Great) (858-67)
Adrian II (867-72)
John VIII (872-82)
Marinus I (882-84)
St Adrian III (884-85)
Stephen VI (885-91)
Formosus (891-96)
Boniface VI (896)
Stephen VII (896-97)
Romanus (897)
Theodore II (897)
John IX (898-900)
Benedict IV (900-03)
Leo V (903)
Sergius III (904-11)
Anastasius III (911-13)
Lando (913-14)
John X (914-28)
Leo VI (928)
Stephen VIII (929-31)
John XI (931-35)
Leo VII (936-39)
Stephen IX (939-42)
Marinus II (942-46)
Agapetus II (946-55)
John XII (955-63)
Leo VIII (963-64)
Benedict V (964)

John XIII (965-72)
Benedict VI (973-74)
Benedict VII (974-83)
John XIV (983-84)
John XV (985-96)
Gregory V (996-99)
Sylvester II (999-1003)
John XVII (1003)
John XVIII (1003-09)
Sergius IV (1009-12)
Benedict VIII (1012-24)
John XIX (1024-32)
Benedict IX (1032-45)
Sylvester III (1045)
Benedict IX (1045)
Gregory VI (1045-46)
Clement II (1046-47)
Benedict IX (1047-48)
Damasus II (1048)
St Leo IX (1049-54)
Victor II (1055-57)
Stephen X (1057-58)
Nicholas II (1058-61)
Alexander II (1061-73)
St Gregory VII (1073-85)
Blessed Victor III (1086-87)
Blessed Urban II (1088-99)
Paschal II (1099-1118)
Gelasius II (1118-19)
Callistus II (1119-24)
Celestine II (1143-44)
Lucius II (1144-45)
Blessed Eugene III (1145-53)
Anastasius IV (1153-54)

Adrian IV (1154-59)
English Pope Nicholas Breakspear, born in Abbots Langley, Herts

Alexander III (1159-81)
Lucius III (1181-85)
Urban III (1185-87)
Gregory VIII (1187)
Clement III (1187-91)
Celestine III (1191-98)
Innocent III (1198-1216)
Honorius III (1216-27)
Gregory IX (1227-41)

Celestine IV (1241)
Innocent IV (1243-54)
Alexander IV (1254-61)
Urban IV (1261-64)
Clement IV (1265-68)
Blessed Gregory X (1271-76)
Blessed Innocent V (1276)
Adrian V (1276)
John XXI (1276-77)
Nicholas III (1277-80)
Martin IV (1281-85)
Honorius IV (1285-87)
Nicholas IV (1288-92)
St Celestine V (1294)
Boniface VIII (1294-1303)
Blessed Benedict XI (1303-04)
Clement V (1305-14)
John XXII (1316-34)
Benedict XII (1334-42)
Clement VI (1342-52)
Innocent VI (1352-62)
Blessed Urban V (1362-70)
Gregory XI (1370-78)
Urban VI (1378-89)
Boniface IX (1389-1404)
Innocent VII (1404-06)
Gregory XII (1406-15)
Martin V (1417-31)
Eugene IV (1431-47)
Nicholas V (1447-55)
Callistus III (1455-58)
Pius II (1458-64)
Paul II (1464-71)
Sixtus IV (1471-84)
Innocent VIII (1484-92)
Alexander VI (1492-1503)
Pius III (1503)
Julius II (1503-13)
Leo X (1513-21)
Adrian VI (1522-23)
Clement VII (1523-34)
Paul III (1534-49)
Julius III (1550-55)
Marcellus II (1555)
Paul IV (1555-59)
Pius IV (1559-65)
St Pius V (1566-72)
Gregory XIII (1572-85)
Sixtus V (1585-90)

Urban VII (1590)
Gregory XIV (1590-91)
Innocent IX (1591)
Clement VIII (1592-1605)
Leo XI (1605)
Paul V (1605-21)
Gregory XV (1621-23)
Urban VIII (1623-44)
Innocent X (1644-55)
Alexander VII (1655-67)
Clement IX (1667-69)
Clement X (1670-76)
Blessed Innocent XI (1676-89)
Alexander VIII (1689-91)
Innocent XII (1691-1700)
Clement XI (1700-21)
Innocent XIII (1721-24)
Benedict XIII (1724-30)
Clement XII (1730-40)
Benedict XIV (1740-58)
Clement XIII (1758-69)
Clement XIV (1769-74)
Pius VI (1775-99)
Pius VII (1800-23)
Leo XII (1823-29)
Pius VIII (1829-30)
Gregory XVI (1831-46)
Blessed Pius IX (1846-78)
Leo XIII (1878-1903)
St Pius X (1903-14)
Benedict XV (1914-22)
Pius XI (1922-39)
Pius XII (1939-58)
Blessed John XXIII (1958-63)
Paul VI (1963-78)
John Paul I (1978)

John Paul II (1978-2005)
In 1982 Pope 'JPII' undertook a six day pastoral visit to the Catholics of the UK

Benedict XVI (2005-present)
Undertook an historic, first state visit to the UK by the Bishop of Rome

Faithful pilgrim

59

In the words of others...

Chief Rabbi, Lord Sacks welcomed Pope Benedict - a leader of a great faith, he said—to the gathering of many faiths, in a land where once battles were fought in the name of faith, and where now we share friendship across faiths. He talked about this as a climate change worth celebrating.

The Chief Rabbi talked about how we celebrate both our commonalities and differences - about how our creative minorities inspire one another and bring our different gifts to the common good - and he talked about how we all believe that faith has a major role in strengthening civil society. In the face of a deeply individualistic culture, he said, we offer community. Against consumerism, we talk about the things that have value but not a price. Against cynicism, we dare to admire and respect. In the face of fragmenting families, we believe in consecrating relationships. We believe in marriage as a commitment, parenthood as a responsibility, and the poetry of everyday life when it is etched, in homes and schools, with the charisma of holiness and grace.

In our communities we value people not for what they earn or what they buy or how they vote, but for what they are, every one of them a fragment of the Divine presence. We hold life holy. And each of us is lifted by the knowledge that we are part of something greater than all of us, that created us in forgiveness and love, and asks us to create in forgiveness and love. The Chief Rabbi said that each of us in our own way is a guardian of values that are in danger of being lost, in our short-attention-span, hyperactive, information-saturated, wisdom-starved age. And though our faiths are profoundly different, yet we recognise in one another the presence of faith itself, that habit of the heart that listens to the music beneath the noise, and knows that God is the point at which soul touches soul and is enlarged by the presence of otherness.

Prime Minister David Cameron spoke to Pope Benedict at the ceremony which brought to a close his four-day visit. He said that the message the Pope had offered was not just for the Catholic Church but to each and every one of us of every faith and none. It is a challenge to us all to follow our conscience, to ask not what are my entitlements, but to ask what our responsibilities are, to ask not what we can do for ourselves, but what we can do for others. The 'common bond of unity' we share, he

said, was an incredibly important part of the Pope's message to us. It is at the heart of the new culture of social responsibility we want to build in Britain.

Mr Cameron said that the Pope had challenged the whole country to sit up and think - and that can only be a good thing. He said that he believes we can all share in the Pope's message of working for the common good and that we all have a social obligation for each other, to our families and our communities. And, he said that, of course, our obligations to each other - and our care for each other - must extend beyond these shores too. Mr Cameron confirmed the agreement he had reached with the Papal delegation following his meeting with them to develop the co-operation between this country and the Holy See on the key international issues where we share a common goal.

Archbishop Vincent Nichols, in his farewell speech to the Holy Father in Birmingham, remarked that Pope Benedict's visit has made both a 'rich contribution' to the history of the nation and will play an important role in 'shaping our future':

'Time and again, you have spoken of the importance of the contribution of the Christian faith in our society, not least because, in your own words, 'if the moral principles underpinning the democratic process are themselves determined by nothing more solid than social consensus, then the fragility of the process becomes all too evident.' We can already sense a new openness to this question; we will pursue and build on these opportunities for the common good of all.

'In speaking to us you have urged young people to find their fulfilment in a love for Christ, a love which will show them that, first, they are loved by Him. That must be true for us too. You have urged our priests to be faithful to their ministry and we bishops to be fathers to our priests. This we will strive to do. You have meditated with us on the 'unity between Christ's sacrifice on the Cross, the Eucharistic sacrifice which he has given to his Church and his eternal priesthood' in which we participate in daily living. Your words point to our baptismal calling 'to bring the reconciling power of his sacrifice to the world in which we live.'

'In this context, you have encouraged us in our work of safeguarding and shown an open heart to those who have suffered through our neglect. For this we thank you. You have reminded us of the importance of sensitive care of the elderly, offered with deep respect and recognition of their spiritual journey. You have reached out to our friends in other faiths, committing us again to work with them and seeking from them an open and reciprocal dialogue. You have led us in prayer and dialogue with our fellow brothers and sisters in Christ, strengthening our friendship and cooperation with them.

'Holy Father, you give us new hearts for the tasks ahead especially in the wonderful gift of declaring John Henry Newman as a blessed model for us to follow…we recognise the importance of the work of fostering vocations and forming men to be the future generations of priests in these countries.

'Holy Father, in this visit you are contributing richly to our history and to the shaping of our future. You lift our hearts and reinvigorate us for our ministry especially in the example you give to us with your openness of heart, keenness of mind and gentle eloquence of expression in your unfailing witness to the mystery of Christ. We take to heart your words that 'we need witnesses of the beauty of holiness, witnesses of the splendour of truth, witnesses of the joy and freedom born of a living relationship with Christ!' This is our calling and we renew our dedication to it today.'

The Archbishop of Canterbury, Rowan Williams, in his speech to Pope Benedict at Lambeth Palace emphasised the need for Christian witness and Christian unity:

'Your Holiness, your consistent and penetrating analysis of the state of European society in general has been a major contribution to public debate on the relations between Church and culture, and we gratefully acknowledge our debt in this respect. Our task as bishops is to preach the Gospel and shepherd the flock of Christ; and this includes the responsibility not only to feed but also to protect it from harm. Today, this involves a readiness to respond to the various trends in our cultural environment that seek to present Christian faith as both an obstacle to human freedom and a scandal to human intellect. We need to be clear that the Gospel of the new creation in Jesus Christ is the door through which we enter into true liberty and true understanding…

'Holiness is at its simplest fellowship with Christ; and when that fellowship with Christ is brought to maturity, so is our fellowship with one another. We must all feel that each of our own ministries is made less by the fact of our dividedness, a very real but imperfect communion. Perhaps we shall not quickly overcome the remaining obstacles to full, restored communion; but no obstacles stand in the way of our seeking, as a matter of joyful obedience to the Lord, more ways in which to build up one another in holiness by prayer and public celebration together, by closer friendship, and by growing together both in the challenging work of service for all whom Christ loves, and mission to all God has made.'

Her Majesty, Queen Elizabeth II, welcomed the Pope in Edinburgh and, in her address, drew attention to the rich tradition of religious freedom in this country and praised the contribution that Christianity has made to world development:

'Your Holiness, your presence here today reminds us of our common Christian heritage, and of the Christian contribution to the encouragement of world peace, and to the economic and social development of the less prosperous countries of the world. We are all aware of the special contribution of the Roman Catholic Church, particularly in its ministry to the poorest and most deprived members of society, its care for the homeless and for the education provided by its extensive network of schools.

'Religion has always been a crucial element in national identity and historical self-consciousness. This has made the relationship between the different faiths a fundamental factor in the necessary cooperation within and between nation states. It is, therefore, vital to encourage a greater mutual, and respectful understanding. We know from experience that through committed dialogue, old suspicions can be transcended and a greater mutual trust established.

'Your Holiness, in recent times you have said that "religions can never become vehicles of hatred, that never by invoking the name of God can evil and violence be justified". Today, in this country, we stand united in that conviction. We hold that freedom to worship is at the core of our tolerant and democratic society.'

 ## Other resources

Heart Speaks Unto Heart: Pope Benedict XVI in the UK - The Complete Addresses and Homilies (2010), Darton, Longman and Todd

Magnificat: Liturgies and Events of the Papal Visit of Pope Benedict XVI to the United Kingdom (2010), Bishops' Conferences of England and Wales and Scotland in co-operation with Gabriel Communications, CTS and Magnificat

Faith Today: Special Papal Souvenir edition (2010), Alive Publishing

For more see http://www.thepapalvisit.org.uk in particular the 'legacy' materials: http://tinyurl.com/papalvisitlegacy. If you have particular interest in reading more on Christian unity http://tinyurl.com/cbcewunity and for more on social justice in the UK visit Caritas Social Action's website http://www.caritas-socialaction.org.uk/

What did you take away from the Pope's visit?

Some have shared their thoughts already...

Jane Kelly from Twyford, Reading
The visit of Pope Benedict was so inspiring and uplifting in every way. I attended both Hyde Park Vigil and Cofton Park and both were amazing events. Heart speaks unto heart was definitely apparent. Wonderful!!!

Joe Williams, Welwyn Garden City
The atmosphere throughout the day was amazing, being among the crowd as we processed through the streets of London was an experience in itself, spontaneous outbreaks of song made it all the more magical.

Marie Kato, Clerkenwell
I will always cherish the Hyde Park vigil in my heart. Aware of our need for the Holy Father's words, it was a moving and humbling privilege to be in the presence of the Pope with close friends and a Church community with whom I share the journey of faith, the love of Christ and a sincere desire to be closer to Him, despite the challenges we face everyday.

We would welcome **your** thoughts by email: marknash@rcdow.org.uk